Grow Your Own

GIANT

Sequoia

Grow Your Own Giant Sequoia

13-Digit ISBN: 978-1-60433-143-1
10-Digit ISBN: 1-60433-143-7
This book may be ordered by mail from the publisher.
Please include $3.50 for postage and handling.
Please support your local bookseller first!

Books published by Cider Mill Press Book Publishers are available at special dis-
counts for bulk purchases in the United States by corporations, institutions, and
other organizations. For more information, please contact the publisher.

Cider Mill Press Book Publishers
"Where good books are ready for press"
12 Port Farm Road
Kennebunkport, Maine 04046

Visit us on the web!
www.cidermillpress.com

Design by Usana Shadday & *the*BookDesigners
Typography Hoefler, Bebas & Marketing Script
Printed in China

1 2 3 4 5 6 7 8 9 0
First Edition

Grow Your Own

GIANT

Sequoia

SCOTT MEYER

TABLE OF **CONTENTS**

A TREE LIKE NO OTHER

Gigantic. *Humongous. Immortal. Beyond your wildest imagination.* When you talk about giant sequoia trees, you can't help but use such extreme terms. They are the largest living things on earth, and they live for thousands of years. They are also rare, growing in the wild only in a limited portion of California's Sierra Nevada Mountains.

Stand in the presence of a mature giant sequoia, and you will find yourself searching for words to describe it. Look up and you'll see that its peak is 250 to 300 feet above you. The lowest branch is more than 100 feet up the trunk, likely higher than the top of any tree you have ever seen. At its widest point, the canopy of branches spreads up to 100 feet in diameter.

Other trees can grow as tall, but the giant sequoia is the biggest because of its volume, a measure of its height and girth combined. Mature sequoias reach at least 35 feet around and some are more than 100 feet in diameter, big enough to drive a car through—which you can actually do in a few spots.

Scientists have determined that giant sequoias were present around the globe back in the days when dinosaurs walked the earth. While no single sequoia has been alive since then, the biggest have been around for more than 3,000 years. They're not just long-lived, they are nearly timeless. Neither old age nor forest fires kill them. The only known causes of death for giant sequoias are lightning strikes and human beings.

Extraordinary size and longevity are not the giant sequoia's only unique features. Its bluish-gray needles and thick, deeply ridged, cinnamon-red bark are similarly striking. Though the big trees are native only in the Sierra Nevadas, they have been planted and are growing well in such diverse places as the Pacific Northwest, the northeastern United States, Great Britain, Italy, and New Zealand.

With the kit that comes with this book, you get seeds that let you grow a living giant sequoia in your own yard and leave it behind for future generations to enjoy. The book explains the tree's ecology, explores its history, and gives you the information you need to plant and grow your own giant sequoia successfully. It also arms you with fascinating facts you can use to amaze friends, family, and others as you plant, tend, and grow your very own natural wonder.

1

The LIFE of a Tree

The Natural History and Ecology of Giant Sequoias

Nearly 200 million years ago, in the era scientists call the Jurassic period, dinosaurs were the dominant animals on earth. At the same time, *Sequoiadendron*, a genus of large trees, were abundant throughout at least the northern half of the planet. The earth is believed to have been much warmer and wetter during the Jurassic period than it is now. There was more carbon dioxide in the atmosphere than today (though research is showing a recent increase in carbon dioxide in the atmosphere). More carbon dioxide produces larger, more robust plants. Fossils of twelve different *Sequoiadendron* species from the Jurassic period have been found in North America, Europe, Greenland, and China.

Then, between 35 and 70 million years ago, the earth experienced major climate change, becoming colder and drier. The era of dinosaurs came to an end, and most of the *Sequoiadendrons* followed them into extinction. Plants better adapted to the new conditions replaced them.

GROWING RANGE

The last of the *Sequoiadendrons* in Europe and Asia disappeared about 20 million years ago, but they survived in North America. About 2 million years ago—the distant past to you and me, but the modern era to geologists—the only remaining member of the

Sequoiadendron genus staked out its current territory on the western slope of the Sierra Nevada Mountains in what is now California. Today, the giant sequoia is found growing wild only in those mountains, in a narrow belt approximately 260 miles long. The northernmost grove is along the middle fork of the American River in Placer County. The southernmost grove is near Deer Creek in Tulare County.

Even in the Sierra Nevada Mountains, the big trees' range is limited. The groves are clustered at an elevation between 4,900 and 8,200 feet above sea level—higher in the southern part of its range, lower as you near the northern end of the range. The healthiest groves are found in protected locations where the average annual precipitation is 45 to 60 inches. The temperature there occasionally drops to −12° F and rarely rises above 100° F. The average growing season lasts from early June to early October. All of these areas have deep soil and consistent moisture provided by snow melt, streams, springs, and fog.

Giant sequoias mostly grow in groves they share with other trees such as white fir, sugar pine, ponderosa pine, incense cedar, and California black oak. Douglas fir, big leaf maple, and canyon live oak also are found in giant sequoia groves. Many different types of shrubs thrive in the shade of the big trees, among them manzanita, Scouler's willow, and western azalea.

ROOTS, BRANCHES, AND BARK

Though giant sequoias have companions in the forest, once they reach maturity, they need plenty of room to spread out and receive unobstructed sunlight. Like many evergreens, they are found in soil that's slightly acidic. The soil tends to be very rich in minerals, the particles left behind when glaciers grind granite and other kinds of rock into dirt.

Under the soil, a sequoia's root system grows up to fourteen feet deep and can spread out over a couple acres—just for a single tree! The huge root system is necessary to support a trunk that can be thirty feet or more in diameter and to gather water for a very thirsty tree. For such large trees, sequoias have a modest amount of branches—the lowest branches on a mature tree are typically 150 feet above the ground. The needles are a blue-tinted green, lance-shaped, overlapping, and cling closely to the twig.

Standing at its base and looking upward, you see that a giant sequoia appears to come to a point. From afar, the top looks cone-shaped. The bark is reddish, has deep grooves, and feels kind of soft. The bark is very thick, up to three feet thick in some cases. Giant sequoias appear to have no insect pests that damage them, leading some entomologists to theorize that tannins in the bark have pest-repellent properties. The bark is also exceptionally fire-resistant—many trees have survived repeated fires. Because the bark is not a good conductor of electricity, lightning strikes are more likely to explode a giant sequoia than burn it. (If a 300-foot-tall tree explodes in the forest and no one is there, does it make a sound? Bet it's quite a big sound!)

LIFE CYCLE

The mighty sequoia tree begins its life as a tiny seed—so tiny that it takes 91,000 seeds to make a pound. Coastal redwood trees, close relatives of the giant sequoia, sprout from roots, stumps, or even fallen logs, just like many other types of trees. But giant sequoias grow only from seeds. Of the thousands of seeds a giant sequoia produces, only about 15 percent of them germinate. The seeds are often carried by the wind—in one case, researchers found seeds 580 feet from the parent tree.

The seeds take root in soil in the ash left behind by a fire rather than in the decaying plant debris found on forest floors. Sequoia seedlings will grow in partial shade, but they rarely establish themselves in the dense grass cover found in meadows, probably because the grass sucks up too much surface moisture while the young tree is trying to build its root system.

Full-grown sequoias aren't troubled by pests, but the seedlings are threatened by sparrows, finches, squirrels, chipmunks, and cutworms in the months after germination. Fungal diseases, notably root rot, and a kind of sunburn called *insolation* can also keep a little sequoia from growing into a giant.

Sequoia seedlings get going at a gradual pace. One-year-old seedlings tend to be about three inches tall. By the end of their second season, they are six inches tall and about double that after the third season. Then the growth rate picks up, and the living giants start to outpace other species. They can be six feet tall by the end of their fourth year and add an inch or two of girth every year. After about 500 years, the growth slows considerably, as they add an inch of diameter only every twenty years or so.

When a giant sequoia finally reaches maturity, at the tender young (for them) age of about 150 to 200 years, they are ready to do what the birds and the bees and all living things do: reproduce. The trees flower in spring and form cone buds in late summer, which are pollinated the following spring. Each tree has both male and female parts (*monoecious*, in scientific terms), so they pollinate themselves.

The egg-shaped, green cones they produce are about two to four inches long. The cones mature but remain green, and the seeds inside become ready to germinate in their second year. A giant sequoia produces on average about 1,500 cones per year. Unlike many other living things, giant sequoias continue the reproduction process as long as they live.

Squirrels, particularly Douglas squirrels, cut down and store mature cones. Few seedlings ever develop from cones buried by squirrels or other animals. The cones that remain on the trees continue to grow, and the seeds inside remain viable (ready to grow) for up to twenty years. A mature tree may have as many 10,000 to 30,000 cones at a time.

Though the growth of these massive trees slows down as it ages, no giant sequoia is known to have died of old age. Fire, insects, diseases—the trees appear to withstand them all and continue growing. If the soil around the tree is persistently disturbed, say by heavy machinery or a landslide, it may blow down. The only creatures capable of halting a giant sequoia's growth are humans.

WHAT'S IN A NAME?

A plant's scientific name is more than something to call it. When botanists name a newly discovered plant (or animal), they are classifying it by its attributes and relating it to other, similar things. Like with people, plants have a family name (genus) and an individual name (species).

The first person to propose a scientific name for the giant sequoia was John Lindley, a professor of botany at the University of London. He got two small living trees, as well as cones and other materials, from a plant collector who had visited the Sierra Madre in the early 1850s. Lindley named the tree *Wellingtonia gigantean,* in honor of the recently deceased Duke of Wellington, who defeated Napoleon at the Battle of Waterloo in 1815.

American botanists were outraged that their native tree had been named for an English war hero, and they proposed numerous alternate names. Among the names were *Taxodium giganteum*, *Washingtonia californica*, *Taxodium washingtonium*, *Sequoia wellingtonia*, and *Sequoia washingtoniana*. Lindley's name was invalidated because *Wellingtonia* had already been used for an unrelated Asian tree. In 1854, Joseph Decaisne, a Belgian botanist and director of the Jardin des Plantes in Paris, identified the giant sequoia as *Sequoia gigantean*. A few years earlier, an Austrian botanist had named the coastal redwood *Sequoia sempervirens*, so the similar-looking giant sequoia was added to the genus.

More than seventy-five years later, a botanist at the University of Illinois, John T. Buchholz, made the case that the giant sequoia and the coastal redwood were different enough to require that they be classified in two different genera. He renamed the giant sequoia as *Sequoiadendron giganteum*, and that is the name used by scientists and botanists around the world today.

Common names can be almost as confusing for nonscientists. Coastal redwoods are similar in size, bark, color, and habitat to giant sequoias, which are also sometimes referred to as Sierra redwoods. *Bigtrees* is another widely used common name for giant sequoias.

IT'S A FACT

Aging gracefully: Sequoia seeds can remain viable for twenty years after they've formed. A dark-red powdery pigment is released with the seeds, and some experts believe this powder protects the seeds until they are ready to germinate.

Fireproof: The bark of a mature sequoia is almost as resistant to flame as asbestos. Many trees have scars from fires, but they keep on living.

Durable: Sequoia trees trunks that have fallen to the ground can remain intact for a thousand years.

2

MAN *Meets* MAMMOTH

The People Who Discovered and Worked to Protect the Big Trees

Although trees related to giant sequoias were thriving on four continents millions of years ago, by the arrival of the first known humans in Europe—an estimated 45,000 years ago—all *Sequoiadendrons* were long gone from the European continent. The only remaining member of the family was the species we know as the giant sequoia, and its range was limited to North America.

The first people to see a giant sequoia growing, then, were very likely the descendents of the migrants who came to North America from Asia about 30,000 years ago. Of course, they left behind no record of their reaction. Undoubtedly, these first North Americans lived in a world that was far wilder and full of more wondrous plants and animals than our own. Yet you have to believe that they were awestruck when they first encountered trees that towered high in the sky above them with trunks much larger than any three of them could reach around.

NATIVE AMERICANS

When Europeans first explored North America, the people living in the foothills on the western side of the Sierra Nevada Mountains among the groves of giant sequoias were from one of two fairly small tribes—the Monache and the Yokuts. In the early 1800s, they numbered about 2,000 people, according to estimates from that time.

The arrival of settlers from the United States during the California Gold Rush of the mid-1800s threatened not only the natives' way of life but their very lives, as disease epidemics and armed conflict dramatically reduced their population. Today, the descendents of the Yokuts and other tribes live on the small Tule River reservation established by a treaty in 1856.

SEQUOYAH, THE MAN

The scientific and common name for the uniquely American tree comes from a unique Native American, a member of the Cherokee tribe who was born about 1770 and died in 1843, just a few years before the world was to learn of the big trees' existence.

Sequoyah reportedly was born in Tennessee to a Cherokee chief's daughter and a fur trader named Nathaniel Gist. The name Sequoyah, or Sikwo-yi, is Cherokee for "pig's foot," which suggests he may have been born with a disability. He fought in the Creek War, an armed conflict between different factions of the tribe in 1813–14) and became a skilled silversmith. But he is best remembered for creating the first system of writing for the Cherokee language. He used 86 letters or symbols to create all the words that make up the Cherokee vocabulary. He first taught the writing system to his daughter, and later he read an argument in a Cherokee court in Chattanooga. Word spread quickly of Sequoyah's invention. In 1821, the Cherokee Nation adopted Sequoyah's system, and in a matter of months, thousands of Cherokee became literate. He then envisioned a common language for all Native American tribes and visited many of them to pursue his lofty but ultimately unrealized dream.

EXPLORERS AND TRAPPERS

Just fifty years after Columbus first crossed the Atlantic, a Portuguese sailor named Juan Rodriguez Cabrillo drafted crude maps of the coast of Alta (Upper) California. Two centuries later, Spain had conquered Mexico and set up twenty-one missions in what is now California, but none of the missions was more than a few dozen miles from the coast. No European had yet explored what Spanish missionary Pedro Font had dubbed the Sierra Nevada, or "snowy mountains." In 1769, Father Crespi, a member of a Spanish expedition, wrote in his diary about the "awesome" trees he had seen but offered no details that inspired anyone to learn more about them. Over the next thirty years, Spanish missionaries and military personnel explored, mapped, and named the valleys and rivers around the mountains where giant sequoias grew, but none recorded an encounter with the trees. In the 1820s, English and French trappers, searching for beavers to supply to the demanding and high-paying fur markets in the eastern United States and Europe, ventured into the Sierra Nevada. The trapping didn't continue for long there—beaver were not as abundant in these mountains as they were in other regions of the West. The trappers moved on without making a single report to the outside world about the huge trees growing in those mountains.

FIRST CONTACTS

In 1833, an explorer from northern California named J. K. Leonard wrote about the big trees in his journal, but he did not state where he saw them. Historians now believe that his route would have taken him through the Calaveras Grove. Leonard made no public announcement of his discovery. Around the same time, John Walker, an explorer searching for a pass through the rugged mountains, also wrote in his journal about the giant sequoia. John Bidwell did the same in 1844. In each of these cases, the findings remained unknown to the public because the journals were not published until years later.

Nearly twenty years later, a homesteader in the Sierra Nevada foothills, John M. Wooster, found the Calaveras

Grove and carved his initials in the bark of one of the trees. Though the initials were visible for decades afterward, he did not publicize his encounter with the big trees, and they still were known only to the few individuals who had seen them in person.

CLEAR EVIDENCE

In the 1850s, the California Gold Rush flooded the region with prospectors and many others seeking to make a living supplying the prospectors. In the spring of 1852, Augustus T. Dowd, a hunter who brought game meat to the miners' camps, hit but did not kill a grizzly bear, so he pursued it into the forest. There he came face-to-trunk with the largest tree he had ever seen, or rather a small grove of trees that dwarfed even the massive coastal redwoods that he probably had seen throughout northern California.

Dowd returned to camp and told the miners about the enormous trunks and skyscraping peaks of the trees. They brushed off his tale as a wild exaggeration. He persisted and a week later, they hiked back to see the trees that had captivated Dowd. They were as amazed as he was. News of the gigantic trees spread first to San Francisco and then to the East Coast. The following year, to Dowd's horror, his tree was cut down and sent in pieces to New York City, where it was reassembled for exhibit. Five men worked for twenty-two days to drop the tree. Tragically, fire destroyed it a year later.

A MAN NAMED MUIR

The promise of riches from gold, silver, and timber attracted many men to the giant sequoia's habitat. John Muir—born in Scotland and raised in Wisconsin—was lured to the Sierra Nevada Mountains by their natural beauty, and he made it his mission to protect the region from degradation by others. He wandered throughout the mountains and canyons, wrote about his travels for newspapers as far away as New York, and was an early and eloquent advocate for creating a national park for the Yosemite Valley. Along the way, he founded the Sierra Club, which is still a leading voice in the conservation movement.

Muir studied geology and botany at the University of Wisconsin, and though he never earned his degree, he was an insightful naturalist. He explored the western flank of the Sierra Nevada and produced the first accurate description of the giant sequoia's range, ecology, and reproductive process. In 1876, the American Association for the Advancement of Science published Muir's paper about the trees. His essay lamented that the grand trees were being destroyed at an irresponsible rate and warned that if they were not soon preserved, the oldest specimens would all be gone forever.

"There is no absolute limit to the existence of any tree," Muir wrote. "Death is due to accidents, not, as that of animals, to the wearing out of organs. Only the leaves die of old age...I never saw one that was sick or showed the slightest sign of decay. Barring accidents, it seems to be immortal."

FROM WONDER TO RESOURCE

A mature giant sequoia yields about 400,000 to 600,000 board feet of lumber, enough to fill 280 freight cars or build 150 homes. The wood is handsome, lightweight, and brittle, and, like the coastal redwood, exceptionally rot-resistant.

The rush to cut down giant sequoias and sell the lumber started just five years after the trees' existence became known to the outside world. Early loggers prepared beds of loose soil and soft branches into which they dropped the trees to help reduce the splitting and splintering that occurred when the giant sequoias hit the ground. The loggers built scaffolds about twelve feet up the trunk and then cut down the trees with welded-together crosscut saws operated by two men.

They often had to use dynamite to break trunks into transportable logs.

In the mid- to late 1800s, many lumber mills were in full operation, and soon acres of giant sequoias were cut down. The lumber was sold for poles, flumes, casks, shingles, and other homebuilding materials. But because the logs were so hard to transport, a lot of trunks were left rotting on the steep hills. The completion of wagon roads and then the development of steam-powered machines accelerated the pace of logging. In 1874, Hyde's Mill, operating on Redwood Mountain near the western boundary of today's Kings Canyon National Park, produced 2 million board feet of lumber, much of it sequoia.

The U.S. Congress, eager to develop the country's natural resources, encouraged the western lumber industry. The Timber and Stone Act, enacted in 1878, allowed any citizen to purchase 160 acres of timberland from the government for $2.50 per acre. Many people took advantage of the opportunity to buy land with giant sequoias either for themselves or to sell to the lumber companies expanding into the region. By the mid-1880s, the Kings River Lumber Company had acquired almost 30,000 acres of timberland near the Grant Grove of giant sequoias. Immediately north of Grant Grove, in Converse Basin between 1892 and 1908, another firm known as Smith and Comstock leveled what is believed to have been the largest giant sequoia grove in existence at the time. Still, the costs of transportation remained so high that no profit was ever made on the timber.

After the establishment of Yosemite, Sequoia, and Kings Canyon National Parks in 1890, most of the biggest sequoia groves were protected from logging. Many years later in 2000, President Bill Clinton designated several outside groves as Giant Sequoia National Monument. That area became the subject of a bitter court battle in 2005–06 between the Bush Administration, the U.S. Forest Service, and the timber industry on one side and the state of California with the Sierra Club on the other. The Bush Administration wanted to open up the area to selective logging. Along with the remaining big trees, environmentalists also expressed concern about the Pacific fisher, a rare member of the weasel family native to the area. In August 2006, U.S. District Judge Charles Breyer of San Francisco blocked the plan, which would have allowed the harvesting of sequoia trees less than thirty inches in diameter. Judge Breyer did not permanently ban commercial lumbering in the southern Sierra Nevada preserve but instead required further study of its environmental impact. The U.S. Forest Service is responsible for the study and must develop a management plan for the giant sequoias within the preserve. So far, no study has been released.

IT'S A FACT ///

The USS *Sequoia* was a yacht used by many American presidents. It is now privately owned.

Mount Sequoyah in the Great Smoky Mountains was named in honor of the father of the Cherokee language.

"Sequoia" is the code name for a new supercomputer due to become operational in 2011.

Stand in the presence of a mature giant sequoia and you will find yourself searching for words to describe it.

3

LAND *of the* GIANTS

How Sequoia National Park Came to Be and What You'll See When You Visit

FUN FACTS AND FASCINATING FIGURES

- On September 25, 1890, U.S. President Benjamin Harrison signed into law a bill protecting many of California's sequoia groves and set up the conditions that led to the establishment of Sequoia National Park. It was the just the second national park in the United States, preceded only by Yellowstone National Park, which was established in 1872. A week later, President Harrison signed bills establishing Yosemite National Park and what is today known as Kings Canyon National Park, both of which contain major sequoia groves.

- When they were first established, the contiguous Sequoia and Kings Canyon National Parks were less than one-ninth of their present size. Over the last century, Congress has made seven major additions to the parks, the last being the Mineral King area in 1978.

- Sequoia National Park today encompasses 864,411 acres, or about three times the area of Los Angeles.

- Within the park are twenty-six sequoia groves covering 7,224 acres. Within those groves are about 35,354 sequoia trees. The Giant Forest grove alone covers 1,800 acres and has 8,400 trees

- The lowest areas of the park, in the foothills of the

Sierra Nevada Mountains, are about 1,300 feet above sea level.

- Mount Whitney, which is visible throughout the park but in fact is in the nearby Inyo National Forest, is 14,491 feet above sea level. It is the tallest peak in the continental United States.

- The park is home to 200 subterranean caverns.

- Kern Canyon in southern Sequoia National Park is 6,000 feet deep, and several of the park's other canyons
are more than 4,000 feet deep. By comparison, the

  average depth of the Grand Canyon in Arizona is about one mile or 5,280 feet.

- More than 1,200 different species of plants have been found in Sequoia National Park.

- The park is home to nearly 300 different species of animals (vertebrates only—not including insects or reptiles). The native wildlife includes the endangered Sierra Nevada bighorn sheep as well as mountain lions, black bear, mule deer, and many creatures unique to this ecosystem.

- The last grizzly bear known to live in California was killed in 1922 in a location close to Sequoia National Park.

- Sequoia and Kings Canyon National Parks contain about 3,200 lakes and ponds and 2,600 miles of rivers and streams.

- Snow covers much of Sequoia National Park from December to May. The average snow depth in late winter is about 40 inches. Winter temperatures rarely drop below 0° F and in summer may reach 100° F.

- The unique, diverse climates and ecosystems in Sequoia and Kings Canyon National Parks collectively earned them designation as an International Biosphere Reserve. Only 531 other areas in the entire world have been so recognized.

- Together, Sequoia and Kings Canyon National Parks protect 265 Native American archeological sites and 69 historic sites.

- Sequoia National Park averages about 1.5 million visitors each year. August is the busiest month.

VISITING THE PARK

Sequoia National Park is one of eight national parks in California. The majority of the park is undeveloped wilderness area—you can hike to a point in the park that is further from a road than any other place in the continental United States. One reason for that is the continual fight conservationists have waged against plans to build cable lifts, golf courses, movie theaters, dance halls, and similar types of attractions that are found in other national parks.

Mid-July to early October are the best times to visit the highest elevations of Sequoia National Park, because the roads and trails are most likely to be snow-free (or at least passable) during those months.

The park's giant sequoia groves are its main draw, with the Giant Forest the most awe inspiring. It is five square miles at an altitude of about 6,500 feet above sea level. This grove includes the General Sherman sequoia, the largest living thing on the planet.

A fun, memorable attraction at Sequoia Natural Park is the Tunnel Log. A sequoia fell across the road in the 1930s, and a hole was cut through the trunk that allows cars to pass beneath it.

Moro Rock is another of the park's natural wonders. It's a solid piece of granite that reaches up 6,725 feet from the valley floor. Visitors are able to climb to the summit because 4,000 steps have been cut into the rock and a railing has been installed.

Climbing to the summit of Mount Whitney is a little more challenging but still possible, even for those without mountaineering experience. Though the mountain itself lies within Inyo National Forest, not Sequoia National Park, you may pick up the High Sierra Trail in the Giant Forest, which you can follow on a six-day hike to the top of the peak. Just be aware that all hikers entering the Mount Whitney zone must obtain a permit.

Far below Mount Whitney and deep beneath the surface of the earth are the 200 caves in Sequoia National Park. The caves are formed out of marble and filled with unique rock formations of all shapes and sizes. You can take a forty-five-minute guided tour of Crystal Cave.

You'll find plenty of lodging options around Sequoia National Park, but Giant Forest Lodge will have you sleeping in the midst of the world's largest trees.

STEWART'S CAMPAIGN

The establishment of a national park cannot be simply attributed to one person, but George W. Stewart was among the first to recognize the need to protect the giant sequoia groves, and he worked persistently to get the public and government to respond. In 1878, Stewart, a first generation Californian, became the city editor of the *Visalia Delta*, a newspaper in a fast-growing mining and logging community in the Sierra Nevada foothills. That year Stewart, only twenty-one years old, wrote an editorial calling for a state law to prohibit the cutting of giant sequoias.

The law was never passed, and before long Stewart shifted the focus of his effort from protecting just the trees to advocating for the establishment of a protectorate over the whole southern Sierra Nevada range. In June 1889, he wrote, "Every acre of unsurveyed timber lands in the Sierra Nevada should be reserved immediately and for all time." Stewart lobbied local businessmen and farmers, organized a petition drive, and pressed the issue with the U.S. Department of the Interior, as well as state and federal political officeholders and candidates. All of these efforts were critical to the passage of the bill establishing Sequoia National Park in 1890.

THE MYSTERIOUS CASE OF H.R. 12187

The behind-the-scenes working of the U.S. Congress in the 1800s was, as it often is now, baffling to outsiders. But the maneuvering that led to the creation of Sequoia National Park as we know it today is still shrouded in the kind of dense fog that settles in the nearby valleys.

A bill listed in the Congressional Record as H.R. 11570 ("H.R." stands for House of Representatives, where the bill originated) was signed on September 25, 1890, by President Benjamin Harrison. This new law preserved about seventy-five square miles of forest, which included one large sequoia grove and another half dozen smaller groves; but it did not specifically designate the area as a national park. Rather, it directed that the land be "set apart as a public park, or pleasure ground, for the benefit and enjoyment of the people..." The law instructed the Interior Department to "provide for the preservation from injury of all timber, mineral deposits, natural curiosities, or wonders within said park, and their retention in their natural state."

Just a week later, President Harrison signed another park bill. This one had been introduced in the House six months earlier as H.R. 8350, with the aim of creating a Yosemite National Park to protect the Yosemite Valley and the Mariposa Grove of giant sequoias. No action had been taken on the bill until after the passage of H.R. 11570. But as the House was preparing to vote on H.R. 8350, a substitute bill, H.R. 12187, was brought to the floor. The original 8350 bill proposed a small federal reservation surrounding the Yosemite state park area; the new bill created a Yosemite National Park that was five times larger than original bill set aside. The substitute bill also contained an entirely new section, which added five townships to

Sequoia National Park and permanently preserved four sections of land surrounding the Grant Grove of big trees.

The bill passed both the House and Senate almost overnight, even though at least one senator objected because he could not understand the bill. (It was not printed, just read on the chambers' floors.) The Yosemite portions of the bill were clear, but the section expanding Sequoia National Park directed only that the added land be "reserved and withdrawn from settlement, occupancy, or sale under the laws of the United States, and...set apart as reserved forest lands..." with no mention of Sequoia National Park or H.R. 11570, which had passed a week earlier. The bill passed the Senate without debate and was signed by President Harrison the following day, October 1, 1890.

Why the mysterious last-minute change? And who was behind it? A few historians have speculated that the Southern Pacific Railroad, the most powerful corporate interest in the region, had a hand in the chain of events, based on a variety of circumstantial evidence. The railroad's motives are linked to its investment in timberland outside the preserve, which would increase in value once the protected areas were no longer open to logging. In addition, the railroad would have expected to benefit from an increase in tourism to the area. In fact, it sent a photographic party to the new

Sequoia National Park during the park's first month of existence.

Whatever the reason or whoever else benefited, we are all able to visit the extraordinary sequoia groves today because of congressional action in September 1890.

CHARLES YOUNG: BARRIER BUSTER

When the new Sequoia National Park was established, Congress tasked the U.S. Army with managing and developing the park. The army had not done much development during the park's first twelve years, but in 1903 a cavalry officer commanding a company of soldiers based at the Presidio in San Francisco was ordered to take his troops to the site for the summer. When Colonel Charles Young and his troopers arrived in Sequoia National Park after a sixteen-day ride, they found that their primary assignment was to extend the wagon road into the forest. The soldiers attacked the job, and within a few months, wagons could enter the mountaintop forest for the first time. In fact, this squad built as much road in one summer season as had been constructed in total over the three previous seasons.

Colonel Young had lots of experience overcoming challenges. He was the first black man to graduate from an all-white high school in Ripley, Ohio, and in 1884 he was appointed to the U.S. Military Academy at West Point. He was only the third black man to graduate with his commission. His assignment to Sequoia National Park made him the first African-American to serve as the superintendent of a U.S. national park.

THE BENEFITS OF FIRE

Though it seems counterintuitive, one of the most important ways that the National Park Service protects giant sequoia trees is by allowing fires to burn in the forest. Yes, let the fires burn. But why?

When fire burns the debris on the forest floor, it creates the mineral-rich soil that giant sequoia seeds grow best in. Fire also causes the cones to open up and release their seeds, so they can germinate. Forest fires also tend to eliminate weaker trees and to reduce the competition from other species that young sequoias must overcome. And, contrary to what you might expect, when periodic fires burn up debris on the forest floor, they reduce the risk of more catastrophic fires that can occur when there is too much fuel to burn. Historically fires have burned in sequoia groves roughly every five to fifteen years.

Today the National Park Service allows naturally occurring fires to burn in Sequoia and Kings Canyon National Parks, unless human life or property are endangered. The park service also employs "prescribed" fires, set and managed by trained experts, to maintain the ecosystem's balance. Most mature giant sequoias bear scars from fires; but if they are healthy, they survive and continue growing to a ripe old age.

The giant sequoia is often confused with the closely related coastal redwood, which can be as tall but not as massive.

4

THE BIGGEST *and the* MOSTEST

The Most Awe-Inspiring Giant Sequoias and Their Astounding Dimensions

THE 10 BIGGEST SEQUOIAS (BY VOLUME)

1. General Sherman, Giant Forest (Sequoia National Park): 274.9 feet tall, 52,508 cubic feet in volume

2. General Grant, Grant Grove (Kings Canyon National Park): 268.1 feet tall, 46,608 cubic feet

3. President, Giant Forest: 240.9 feet tall, 45,148 cubic feet

4. Lincoln, Giant Forest: 255.8 feet tall, 44,471 cubic feet

5. Amos Alonzo Stagg, Alder Creek Grove (Sequoia National Park): 243 feet tall, 42,557 cubic feet

6. Boole, Converse Basin (Sequoia National Park): 268.8 feet tall, 42,509 cubic feet

7. Genesis, Mountain Home Grove (Mountain Home Demonstration State Forest, Porterville, California): 253 feet tall, 41,900 cubic feet

8. Franklin, Giant Forest: 223.8 feet tall, 41,280 cubic feet

9. King Arthur, Garfield Grove (Sequoia National Park): 270.3 feet tall, 40,656 cubic feet

10. Monroe, Giant Forest: 247.8 feet tall, 40,177 cubic feet

SUPER SEQUOIAS

- Tallest: 311 feet, unnamed tree, Redwood Mountain Grove

- Oldest: 3,500 years or more, various trees in Converse Basin, Mountain Home Grove, and Giant Forest

- Greatest Girth: 155 feet, Waterfall Tree. Alder Creek Grove

- Largest Limb: 12.8 feet in diameter, Arm Tree, Atwell Mill, East Fork Grove

WALK-THROUGH/RIDE-THROUGH

Fire burned a hole big enough to ride a horse through the Wishbone Tree in Mountain Home Demonstration State Forest. In earlier days, a park road passed through this tree.

The Wawona Tunnel Tree in Yosemite National Park was 227 feet tall and 90 feet in circumference. In 1881, two men were hired to enlarge an existing fire scar into a tunnel. The tree became a popular tourist attraction. It was photographed with horse-drawn carriages rolling through it and later cars. In 1969, a two-ton load of snow on its crown toppled the roughly 2,300-year-old sequoia.

GENERAL SHERMAN TREE

One of John Muir's companions in his exploration of the Sierra Nevada Mountains was James Wolverton, who had served on the Union side in the Civil War under General William Tecumseh Sherman. When Wolverton found the most massive sequoia in the Giant Forest in 1879, he named it after his former commander.

The General Sherman is considered the world's biggest tree, though it is neither the tallest nor the widest. Its volume, however, is unequaled. (Calculating the volume of a living tree has been likened to measuring the volume of an irregular cone.) It weighs about as much as 10 blue whales.

Here are the tree's vital statistics:

> **Weight:** 2.7 million pounds
> **Height:** 274.9 feet
> **Circumference at ground level:** 102.6 feet
> **Diameter of the largest branch:** 6.8 feet
> **Approximate age:** 2,300 to 2,700 years
> **Lowest limb:** 130 feet above ground

AMERICA'S CHRISTMAS TREE

The General Grant Tree, the world's second largest giant sequoia, is nearly 270 feet tall, 108 feet in circumference, and estimated to be almost 2,000 years old. In 1924, Charles E. Lee, a member of the Sanger, California, Chamber of Commerce, was visiting General Grant National Park (now Kings Canyon National Park). As legend has it, Lee was looking up at the General Grant Tree when he heard a little girl say, "What a wonderful Christmas tree it would be!"

The next year, Lee organized a Christmas day celebration at the site of the tree, and a few months later, he successfully lobbied President Calvin Coolidge to designate the General Grant as the "Nation's Christmas Tree." Thirty years later, President Dwight D. Eisenhower proclaimed the General Grant Tree to be a national shrine. The tree is America's only living shrine. Eisenhower also dedicated the Nation's Christmas Tree to serve as a living memorial to honor fallen war heroes. Each year on Christmas Day, a wreath is placed at the base of the tree in remembrance of those who gave their lives serving their country.

GIANT HUNTERS

Wendell Flint, a World War II veteran and later a high-school math teacher living in Coalinga, California, scoured the groves and canyons of the Sierra Nevada for more than forty years, searching for a sequoia bigger than the General Sherman. From 1967 until Flint passed away in 2002, he was joined on his quest by Mike Law, an artist and Vietnam War veteran.

Flint and Law followed tips and leads, and they discovered many significant sequoias. They painstakingly measured sixty-one other giants and added their whereabouts to the list of noteworthy trees. They measured and named, among others, the Genesis, the Diamond, and Three-Fingered Jack trees.

In 1987, The Sequoia Natural History Association published Flint's book, *To Find the Biggest Tree*, which also featured Law's photographs. The book included the measurements they made of the thirty-four largest sequoias. It reiterated the findings of the engineers who determined in 1931 that the General Sherman is the largest tree on earth (by volume).

IT'S A FACT

- Mature giant sequoias are as tall as an average twenty-six-story building.

- At its base, the circumference of a mature giant sequoia is wider than many city streets.

- A growing giant sequoia produces about forty cubic feet of new wood each year.

5

RAISING YOUR OWN *Big Tree*

Everything You Need to Know to Grow Your Own Giant Sequoia from Seeds

You are about to make history. Or at least leave behind a legacy that will endure for centuries to come. Planting a tree, any kind of tree, is a gift you give to the future. But starting a giant sequoia and watching it begin growing to its full potential is also fun and rewarding right now. You get to see the miraculous transformation of small, ordinary-looking seeds into what will one day become a living behemoth.

The seeds that come with this book contain all the genetic information they need to become the biggest and oldest living things on earth. In the next few pages, you'll get all the information you need to start your giant sequoia off strong and healthy and prepare it for a long and happy life. As you nurture the small tree and invest your time and effort in it, remember that you are trying to work with nature and not force it to bend to your will. Whenever you have a choice to make, go the natural route, take a pass on the chemicals. You will make the world more sustainable and leave the planet a healthier place for your giant sequoia—and your descendents.

PREP THE SEEDS

In its native habitat, a giant sequoia always starts as a seed—it never sprouts up as a shoot from an existing tree. Giant sequoia seeds are released and germinate when high temperatures (typically but not exclusively from forest fires) force open the cones where the seeds are formed. Exposure to heat also "scarifies" the seed, which means to thin or crack its hard outer coat, which allows air and moisture to get inside to the seedling embryo.

The first part of that process has already been taken care of—otherwise you'd be holding a nice green cone in your hand! You may, however, have to assist with scarifying the seeds. Don't worry—no special tools or knowledge of botany is needed. Take either a metal file or a piece of fine grade sandpaper and rub each seed a few times, enough to create a permeable spot on the seed. Test your results by dropping a few seeds in a dish of water. If they sink after a few minutes, you scarified them right and you can plant them. If they float, they're still watertight. Try again, but be sure you don't rub so hard that you remove the seed coat completely.

INDOOR START

In ideal conditions—like the western slope of the Sierra Nevada Mountains—you can with confidence plant your Giant Sequoia seeds directly into the ground. In most other locations, though, you'll want to start the seeds in pots and then transplant them to their final home when they have grown into saplings.

Growing seeds into saplings is not hard. You plant the seeds in small pots like the one included with this book. Start them off with good soil, follow a simple watering and feeding plan, put them under lights you can buy at any hardware store, and in three to four months you will have a thin stem and root system ready to move into a bigger pot. In six to eight months, your sapling will be sturdy enough to move into the ground—in friendly conditions. In most parts of the United States, early autumn is the best time to plant trees. Start your seeds in winter and they'll be ready just in time for fall. The very first step is getting the proper soil to plant in.

MIX YOUR MEDIUM

The soil you dig up from your yard is not the best environment in which to start any kind of seed in a pot, including Giant Sequoias. The soil tends to be too dense, so it holds more water than the seeds need, which can cause them to rot. Rather, you want a blend of loose material, such as sphagnum peat moss or coir (the fibrous hairs left behind when coconuts are processed); perlite, a mineral that helps to disperse moisture evenly; and balanced, well-aged compost (not composted cow manure). If you want to make this blend yourself, the ratios are three parts peat or coir to one part perlite and two parts compost. You can also buy "soilless" mix in bags at many garden centers and hardware stores. Just be sure to avoid mixes with synthetic fertilizers – they act like anabolic steroids do in people, causing unnatural growth that leaves the plant vulnerable to disease.

Pots like the one that came with this book are made from much the same materials as your soilless mix— they are formed from peat or coir. They work well because they let you transplant the whole pot without disturbing the roots. Get 19 more pots just like the one you already have, so you'll have one for each of your seeds. (You can find these fiber pots at garden centers or online.)

SOW THE SEEDS

Put the soil mix in a bucket and moisten it thoroughly. You don't want it to be soggy, just a shade past damp—like a sponge that's been wrung out. Fill each pot nearly full with the mix. Push one seed into the soil, about one-half inch deep. Cover the seeds lightly with the soil mix, but don't pat it down too hard.

You need to keep the soil consistently moist (again, not soggy) while you wait for the seeds to germinate, which can take up to 21 days or even longer after planting. The plastic "greenhouse" that came with the book helps to maintain a high humidity level around the pot. For the other pots, you can cover them with clear plastic (like a dry cleaning bag or food wrap) or place them in a plastic tray with a clear lid. Just be sure not to let so much condensation build up on it that fungus starts growing, which can kill your sequoia seedling. If you see mold or other fungus in the pot, sprinkle a little dry peat moss or ordinary cornmeal on top of the soil.

Place the pots in a warm, but not hot, location. At this stage, you do not need to provide them with light.

NURTURE THE SEEDLING

As soon as you see sprouts coming up through the soil, remove the plastic. You still need to keep the soil damp, but too much humidity can cause the sprouts to rot.

The sprouts now need light. If you have a window that faces south or west (the directions that get the most hours of sunlight), place the pots as close as you can to it without touching it. If you don't have a window that gets sufficient light, you can use ordinary fluorescent shop lights, which you can get at most home centers and hardware stores. (You don't need expensive grow lights for this.) Place the seedlings a couple inches from the lights—fluorescent bulbs don't get hot so this won't burn your little trees-to-be. As the seedlings grow, keep them 2 to 3 inches from the lights. Leave the lights on them at least 10 hours a day, up to 14 if you can.

Just like when they were germinating, your tree seedlings need consistent moisture to continue growing. Try as best you can to moisten the soil rather than pouring water on the tender seedling.

When the seedlings are about a month old and have a couple sets of leaves, they are ready for a little fertilizing. Use a very diluted solution of liquid seaweed and fish, an organic fertilizer sold in garden centers and nurseries. Don't make it too strong—like in people, overfeeding is unhealthy for plants, even those that will someday be giant trees. Feed the seedlings like this every other weeks until you plant them outside.

MOVE ON UP

When the seedlings become too top heavy for their pots, they're ready for a bigger home. The ideal pots for this purpose are large (10 gallon is best) and have drainage holes. Since these pots are only a temporary home, you don't need decorative or even attractive containers. Basic plastic works fine, though you can use terra cotta, if you prefer. (Just bear in mind that terra cotta pots dry out faster than plastic, so you need to be

especially attentive to watering seedlings in clay pots.)
Look for plastic pots like these at nursery supply outlets
online or in your community.

Your soil mix for these pots will have the same
ingredients as you used to start the seeds, but increase
the amount of compost so that it is roughly equal to
the amount of peat or coir. Keep the same proportion
of perlite or vermiculite. Like you did when you were
starting the seeds, moisten the soil before filling the
pots with it.

Dig a hole in the soil in each container the depth and
width of your little pots. Pick up each little pot and
gently tear it and separate it from the soil inside at two
or three spots. Be careful not to rip the roots--if you
encounter any resistance, stop. Place the tree into the
hole so that the stem is at exactly the same depth as it
was in the little pot. No deeper or you may smother the
roots.

Continue to keep the seedlings close to the lights. As
the weather warms during the spring and summer,
you can bring the large pots outside during the day.
Start them off outside in a shady area, then move them
into filtered sunlight, and eventually into full sun.
Remember to keep the soil consistently moist—sunlight
dries out the soil mix very quickly.

FIND THE RIGHT SITE ///

The most critical choice you make for your giant sequoia is the location where you will plant it. Sequoias grow in the wild in a very specific place for a reason—because the place has the conditions that are most hospitable for them. Your goal, then, is to find a spot that shares some key characteristics with the conditions in the Sierra Nevada Mountains.

First, be sure the site you choose has enough space for the tree's root system, which will at maturity reach 12 to 14 feet deep and spread to more than one acre. Don't plant them in locations where the roots can damage or be hampered by underground water or sewage systems. Also, be sure the tree won't be shaded in its early years by nearby buildings or other trees and shrubs. Giant sequoias grow fastest when they get all-day sunlight.

Second, giant sequoias thrive in soil that is consistently moist through most of the year but not soggy. Avoid spots that are always muddy—the saplings will literally drown in them. On the other hand, planting in an area that stays bone-dry most of the year will require you to irrigate the young tree nearly every day, which is both a lot of work and wasteful.

BUILD THE SOIL

The most important effort you can put into growing any plant, including trees, is soil building. The soil where giant sequoias grow on their own is rich in minerals and has a slightly acidic pH. As we already discussed, the soil should hold some moisture but not be so dense that it stays soggy all the time.

You can get a simple, low-cost soil test from your state's cooperative extension service (there is an office in just about every county in the United States), or you can buy a home test kit, which typically measures only the pH. Lab test results tell you the pH; whether you have sufficient levels of major nutrients, such as phosphorus, potassium, magnesium, and calcium; and the amount of organic matter in the soil (5 percent is ideal). With that information, you can buy the right "amendments" online or at your local garden center to mix into the soil to get the nutrients up to their proper levels. If the soil is too acidic (below 5.5), you can add lime to raise it. Where the soil is too alkaline (higher than 7.5), you can apply sulfur. Just bear in mind that the most alkaline soils (generally found in very dry climates like the Southwest) are very difficult to permanently alter, because limestone and similar bedrock continually break down and raise the soil's pH.

The soil where giant sequoias grow naturally is always replenished with organic matter because it comes from the decaying needles, bark, and other stuff that falls from the tree itself and from surrounding plants. This organic matter feeds a whole food chain in the soil, including bacteria, fungi, and larger creatures like worms that break it down into the nutrients the trees feed on. You can mimic this process for your giant sequoias by mixing in compost—bought or homemade—before you plant trees and adding a half-inch layer on top of the soil at least once per season (more often in hotter, drier climates).

TRANSPLANT YOUR SAPLINGS

In most areas of North America, the ideal time to plant a tree is in early autumn. The temperatures are moderate, the air is moist but not suffocatingly humid, most pests and weeds have completed their life cycle for the year, and the trees have time to start building a root system before winter. You can also plant trees after the ground has dried out in spring, before summer heat sets in.

Your giant sequoia saplings will be ready for transplanting outside when they get to be at least six inches tall. About two to three weeks before you are ready to transplant them, you want to put them through a process known as "hardening off." Take the pots outside for a few hours each day at first, so they adjust to the sunlight, wind, and other conditions. Bring them in each night, but gradually increase the amount of time they are outside until you are leaving them out all day.

When you are ready to plant, dig a hole that is about as deep as the container and about three times the diameter. Scrape the sides of the hole a bit so that roots can attach themselves to the rough spots and grow into the surrounding soil. This is especially critical in heavy clay soil. Moisten the soil in the hole.

Turn the pot over to remove the sapling. Push gently from the bottom if it doesn't slide right out—don't pull it out by the stem, which could cause it to break off. Giant sequoia roots are very brittle, so leave the soil attached to them and be careful to avoid breaking even the smallest roots.

Set the sapling in the hole and gently backfill with the soil you dug out. Mix compost in with the soil. Don't press on the soil/compost mixture because you don't want to squeeze out all the air pockets. Around the stem, form the soil into a small bowl to help direct water to the roots that are directly beneath the stem. Water lightly to settle the sapling in, then cover the exposed soil with an inch or so of dried grass clippings, shredded fall leaves, or straw to keep the soil moist and weeds from sprouting up.

If you are planting more than one giant sequoia, you can place them as close as six feet apart to create a windbreak or use them as a privacy screen. To grow a real giant, though, you want to leave at least thirty feet between them.

WATER AND FEED

In case it hasn't been made clear enough yet, giant sequoias need constant, even moisture to grow well, especially during their first year. Pay careful attention to them and never let the soil dry out. In the first month or two, you may need to water them every day or every other day during rain-free spells. After that, you can give them a deep drenching just once a week. Maintain a layer of mulch—dried grass clippings, straw, shredded leaves, or bark nuggets—on top of the soil at all times. This both keeps the sun from drying out the top few inches of soil and blocks weeds, which suck up moisture before it reaches your tree's roots.

Compost is the best fertilizer for your giant sequoias because it is how nature feeds them. Spread a half-inch layer on top of the soil (beneath the mulch layer) once or twice a year, and it will provide all of the nourishment your growing giant needs. If you have no access to compost, use a balanced (5-5-5), slow-release organic fertilizer. Synthetic fertilizers not only cause unnatural, unsustainable growth, they also are high in salts that dry out the soil and harm the helpful underground microbes.

PROTECT IN WINTER

Giant sequoias in their natural habitat are surrounded by snow all winter, but it is not a frigid climate. In fact, the snow acts as insulation, protecting the young trees and their roots from crippling hard freezes.

If you live where winter temperatures stay well below freezing and the snow cover is not consistent, protect younger trees (less than five years old) by wrapping them loosely in burlap or just covering them with a box during the coldest spells. Wherever you live, remember to keep

younger trees hydrated until the ground freezes solid, at which point they go into dormancy.

When they are less than five years old, some giant sequoias turn a rust, brown, or bronze shade after a cold snap and a dry spell. Don't worry about this—they will return to their normal light brown color when they are watered and warm weather returns. In very hot weather, the needles may turn yellow and even fall off. In both cases, older trees are less likely to be stressed by temperature swings.

LOOK FORWARD

Giant sequoias are among the fastest growing trees. In ideal conditions, they add six feet of height and an inch or two of diameter every year after their third year. A giant sequoia planted in Italy reportedly reached seventy-two feet in height after only seventeen years. Even if your trees don't grow at that pace, before long they will be the biggest plants in your yard.

GROW A BONSAI SEQUOIA

Don't have enough room or a permanent place where you can plant a giant sequoia? Try using one to make into bonsai, the traditional Asian art of training trees in pots to create a natural-looking, miniature landscape.

Many books, websites, and instructors can provide you with detailed information on how to practice the art of bonsai. With giant sequoias, you still must be sure to give the tree consistent moisture, even in a bonsai pot. Don't think that you can keep the tree small by withholding the water or fertilizer that giant sequoias need to stay healthy and strong. Focused pruning of both branches and roots is the only way to manage a bonsai sequoia's size.

Done right, almost any bonsai plant can become a family heirloom. Trees as long-lived as a giant sequoia, grown in a bonsai pot or in the ground, are certain to be enjoyed for many generations.

IT'S A FACT

The cooling effect of a healthy tree is equal to ten room-size air conditioners operating twenty hours a day, according to the U.S. Department of Agriculture.

Th he best time to plant a tree was twenty years ago. The next best time is today."
—Chinese proverb

RESOURCES
Where to Learn More

TO LEARN MORE ABOUT GIANT SEQUOIAS AND THEIR HISTORY

Sequoia Natural History Association
www.sequoiahistory.org

Challenge of the Big Trees
an online book by Larry M. Dilsaver and William C. Tweed,
hosted by the National Park Service
www.nps.gov/history/history/online_books/dilsaver-tweed/
contents.htm

Forest Service Manual, by the U.S. Department of Agriculture
www.na.fs.fed.us/pubs/silvics_manual/volume_1/
sequoiadendron/giganteum.htm

To Find the Biggest Tree, by Wendell Flint and Mike Law
(published by Sequoia Natural History Association in 2002)

TO GET MORE INFORMATION ABOUT GROWING AND CARING FOR YOUR TREES

Giant Sequoia and Redwood Tree Landscape Nursery
Auberry, California
www.giant-sequoia.com

The International Society of Arboriculture
www.treesaregood.com

The National Arbor Day Foundation
www.arborday.org

TreeHelp.com
www.treehelp.com

TO SEE AWESOME PHOTOS OF GIANT SEQUOIAS

Humboldt State University Photo Tour
www.humboldt.edu/~sillett/sequoia.html

Tree Pictures
www.tree-pictures.com/sequoia_tree_pictures.html

TO HELP PRESERVE AND PROTECT OUR NATURAL RESOURCES

The Sierra Club
www.sierraclub.org

The Nature Conservancy
www.nature.org

TO VISIT SEQUOIA NATIONAL PARK AND KINGS CANYON NATIONAL PARK

National Park Service
www.nps.gov/seki/

National Park Vacations
www.visitsequoia.com/

GROWING NOTES

Seeds planted...

First sprout..

First set of true leaves...

Transplanted to larger pot...

Transplanted outside...

Height when transplanted...

5 feet tall...

10 feet tall...

20 feet tall...

50 feet tall...

100 feet tall...

200 feet tall...

Fertilized..

....

....

....

....

....

....

....

You find this information, which is specific to your area, online or by calling your county's extension office.

Average first frost date...

....

Average last frost date...

....

Annual low temperature...

....

Annual high temperature.......................................

....

Average rainfall...

....

Soil pH...

....

ABOUT CIDER MILL PRESS BOOK PUBLISHERS

Good ideas ripen with time. From seed to harvest,
Cider Mill Press brings fine reading, information,
and entertainment together between the covers of
its creatively crafted books. Our Cider Mill bears
fruit twice a year, publishing a new crop of titles
each Spring and Fall.

Visit us on the web at
www.cidermillpress.com
or write to us at
12 Port Farm Road
Kennebunkport, Maine 04046